USBORNE

FRENCH SONGBOOK

Anthony Marks and Sylvestre Balazard

Designed by Joanne Pedley
Illustrated by Simone Abel
Edited by Nicole Irving

Arrangements by Anthony Marks and Sylvestre Balazard
With thanks to Renée Chaspoul

Contents

Un, deux, trois, 3
Au clair de la lune, 4
Sur le pont d'Avignon, 6
Vendôme, 7
Alouette, 8
Le coucou, 9
À la claire fontaine, 10
J'ai descendu dans mon jardin, 11
Fais dodo, 12
Dimanche matin, 13
La capucine, 14
Savez-vous planter les choux? 15
Promenons-nous dans les bois, 16
Le furet, 17
Frère Jacques, 18
Meunier, tu dors, 19
Cadet Rousselle, 20
Il pleut, il pleut, bergère, 22
Trois jeunes tambours, 24
Il est né, le divin enfant, 26
Les trois rois, 28
Word list, 30
Singing French songs, 32

About this book

The songs in this book are all well-known French nursery rhymes, children's songs, folk songs or carols. Each one has been carefully arranged for children's voices, with simple parts for piano or keyboard. The top line can be played on a recorder or other melody instrument. There are also chord symbols for guitarists; these are explained on page 32.

Each song contains the words in the original French, as well as a pronunciation guide. By reading the guides as if they were English words, singers with little experience of French will be able to sound convincing in the language. In this way, even very young children will quickly become familiar with the way French words sound.

Every song is accompanied by a detailed explanation of its meaning, and a translation of its most important words and phrases. There is also a comprehensive vocabulary list on pages 30 and 31, and further information about pronunciation on page 32.

Un, deux, trois
One, two, three

Singing this song will help you remember how to count up to twelve in French. It is about picking cherries.

Allons dans les bois means "Let's go into the woods".

Cueillir des cerises means "to pick cherries".

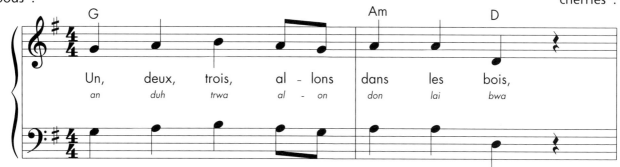

G   Am   D

Un,   deux,   trois,   al - lons   dans   les   bois,
an   *duh*   *trwa*   *al - on*   *don*   *lai*   *bwa*

G   Am   D   G

Quatre, cinq,   six,   cueil - lir   des   ce - rises,   Sept,   huit,   neuf,   dans mon
katr   *san*   *seece* *kuh - yeer*   *dai* *suh - reese*   *set*   *weet*   *nuhf*   *don   mon*

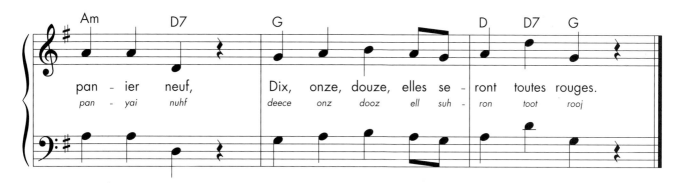

Am   D7   G   D   D7   G

pan - ier   neuf,   Dix, onze, douze, elles se - ront toutes rouges.
pan - yai   *nuhf*   *deece* *onz*   *dooz*   *ell* *suh - ron*   *toot*   *rooj*

Dans mon panier neuf means "in my new basket".

Elles seront toutes rouges means "they'll all be red".

In French, this sort of counting rhyme is called a *comptine*.

Au clair de la lune

In the moonlight

This song was written in the 17th century. Some people think it is by Jean-Baptiste Lully, a famous French composer. A Pierrot is a type of clown, with a white face and a black cap.

① Late one night, the singer knocks on his friend Pierrot's door, asking to borrow a pen.

② He wants to write a letter, but his candle has blown out.

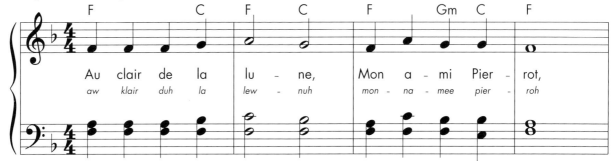

Au clair de la lu - ne, Mon a - mi Pier - rot,
aw klair duh la lew - nuh mon - na - mee pier - roh

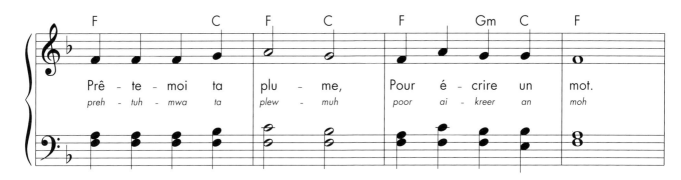

Prê - te - moi ta plu - me, Pour é - crire un mot.
preh - tuh - mwa ta plew - muh poor ai - kreer an moh

Ma chan - delle est mor - te, Je n'ai plus de feu.
ma shon - dell ai mor - tuh juh nai plew duh fuh

Ou - vre - moi ta por - te, Pour l'a - mour de Dieu.
oo - vruh - mwa ta por - tuh poor la - moor duh deeuh

Au clair de la lune, Pierrot répondit:
aw klair duh la lew-nuh pier-roh rai-pon-dee
"Je n'ai pas de plume, Je suis dans mon lit.
juh nai pa duh plew-muh juh swee don mon lee
Va chez la voisine, Je crois qu'elle y est,
va shai la vwa-zee-nuh juh crwa kel ee ai
Car dans la cuisine, On bat le briquet."
car don la kwee-zee-nuh on ba luh bree-kai

③ Pierrot replies that he is in bed, and doesn't have a pen.

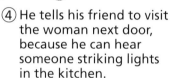

④ He tells his friend to visit the woman next door, because he can hear someone striking lights in the kitchen.

A *briquet* was a piece of metal that made sparks to light fires and candles. (*Briquet* is also the word for a lighter.)

Au clair de la lune, Pierrot se rendort,
aw klair duh la lew-nuh pier-roh suh ron-dor
Il rêve à la lune, son coeur bat bien fort:
eel rev a la lew-nuh son kuhr ba byan for
Car toujours si bonne, Pour l'enfant tout blanc
car too-joor see bon-nuh poor lon-fon too blon
La lune lui donne son croissant d'argent.
la lew-nuh lwee don-nuh son krwa-son dah-jon

⑤ Pierrot goes back to sleep, and dreams of the moon.

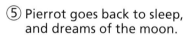

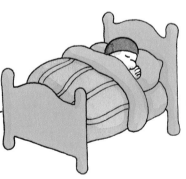

Pierrot is described as *l'enfant tout blanc* because of his white face and costume.

Pierrot first became popular as a character in a type of Italian pantomine.

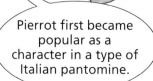

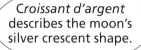

Croissant d'argent describes the moon's silver crescent shape.

Sur le pont d'Avignon

On the bridge at Avignon

Avignon is a town in Provence, in the south of France. There is a bridge across the River Rhône there that was built hundreds of years ago. Only half of it is left now. There are some actions for the second part of the song.

When you sing *Les beaux messieurs*, all the boys bow.

When you sing *Et les belles dames*, all the girls curtsy.

Sur le pont
sewr luh pon
d'A – vi – gnon
da – vee – nyon
On y dan – se,
on – nee don – suh

on y dan – se
on – nee don – suh
Sur le pont
sewr luh pon
d'A – vi – gnon
da – vee – nyon

On y dan – se
on – nee don – suh
tout en rond.
too – ton ron
Fine
Les beaux me – ssieurs font
lai bo mess – yuh fon

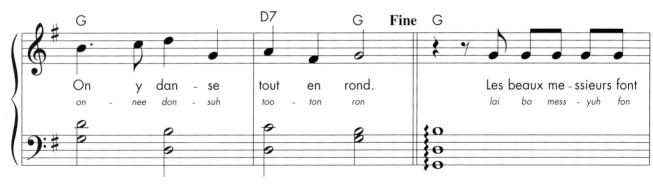

comme ça
kom sa
Et les belles dames font
ai lai bell dam fon
comme ça.
kom sa

D.C. al fine

Vendôme

Vendôme

Vendôme is a town in central France. The song is about King Charles VII of France, and his fight to win back lands that had been lost in a war with the English.

Dauphin is the title given to a prince who will one day become king.

Dauphin is also the word for a dolphin.

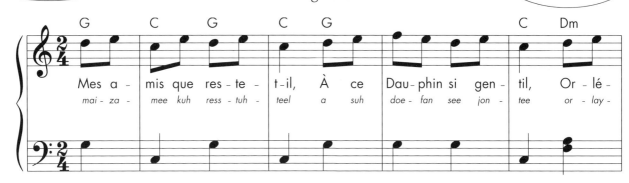

Mes a- mis que res- te- t- il, À ce Dau- phin si gen- til, Or lé-
mai- za- mee kuh ress- tuh- teel a suh doe- fan see jon- tee or- lay-

- ans, Beau- gen- cy, No- tre Da- me de Clé- ry, Ven- dô- me, Ven- dô- me.
- on bo- jon- see noh- truh dam- muh duh clai- ree von- dom- uh von- dom- uh

Even after his father died in 1422, Charles VII was still known as *le Dauphin*. He was not really king of France, as most of his land had been taken by the English.

The song mentions four towns that belonged to him. They are shown on the map below. Slowly he won back most of France.

He was helped by a woman called Jeanne d'Arc, who persuaded a large army to fight for him.

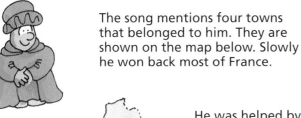

In 1429, *le Dauphin* was crowned king of the whole of France at a ceremony in Reims. He ruled France until he died in 1461.

Alouette

The skylark

The singer is trying to catch a skylark. *Gentille alouette, je te plumerai la tête* means "Sweet skylark, I'll pluck the feathers on your head".

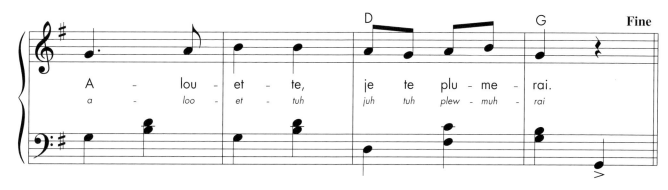

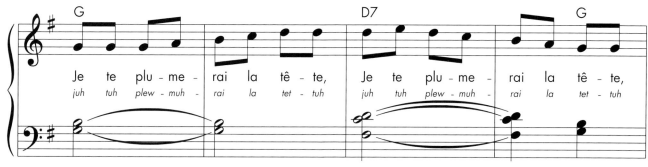

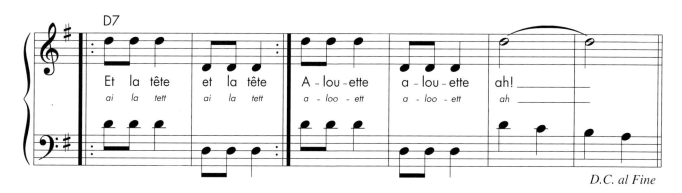

D.C. al Fine

8

Le coucou

The cuckoo

In this song there are imitations of a cuckoo's call.
Dans la forêt lointaine means "in the distant forest".
Un chêne is an oak tree, and *un hibou* is an owl.

You can sing this tune as a round. Find out more below.

Dans la fo - rêt loin - tai - ne, On en - tend le cou -
don la fo - rai lwan - ten - nuh on on - ton luh coo -

- cou. Du haut de son grand chê - ne, Il ré - pond au hi -
- coo dew o duh son gron shen - nuh eel rai - pon - toe ee -

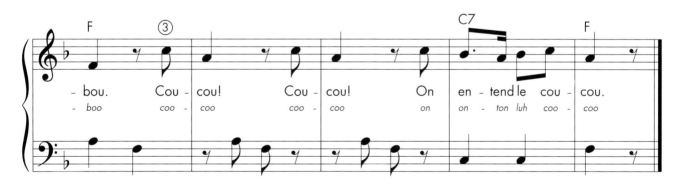

- bou. Cou - cou! Cou - cou! On en - tend le cou - cou.
- boo coo - coo coo - coo on on - ton luh coo - coo

You need three people, or three groups, to sing *Le coucou* as a round.

The first person or group starts at the beginning.

When they reach the number 2 in the music, the second person starts at the beginning.

When the first person gets to the number 3, the third singer starts.

À la claire fontaine

By the clear fountain

The words to this song come from France, but the tune is Canadian. It comes from Quebec, an area of Canada where most people speak French.

The singer goes for a walk one day to a spring. The water looks so beautiful that he climbs into it.

He thinks about the woman he has loved for a long time, and says he will never forget her.

À la clai-re fon-tai-ne, M'en al-lant pro-me-ner,
a la kleh-ruh fon-ten-nuh, mon al-lon pro-muh-nai

J'ai trou-vé l'eau si bel-le, Que je m'y suis bai-gné.
jai troo-vai law see bell-uh kuh juh mee swee benn-yai

Il y a long-temps que je t'aime, Ja-mais je ne t'ou-blie-rai.
eel ya lon-ton kuh juh tem-muh ja-may juh nuh too-blee-rai

French people first went to live in Canada in the 17th century.

The city of Quebec was founded by Samuel de Champlain, a French explorer, in 1608.

Later, the French areas of Canada were taken over by the English. This song became very popular among French Canadians, who sang it to remember France.

CANADA
Quebec
Quebec City
USA

J'ai descendu dans mon jardin

I went down into my garden

This is a very old French song. *Romarin* is the French word for rosemary, a herb that is often used in cooking.

The singer went down into her garden to pick some rosemary.

She found some pretty new poppies growing there.

J'ai descendu is an old-fashioned way of saying "I went down". People do not say this today.

The correct French is *Je suis descendu* for a man, and *Je suis descendue* for a woman.

Fais dodo

Go to sleep

There are lots of childish words in this lullaby. *Dodo* is short for *dormir* (to sleep), and *Colas* is short for the name Nicolas. *Lolo* means *lait* (milk), and *lola* is short for *chocolat* (chocolate).

The singer tells her little brother to go to sleep, and promises him some milk.

Their mother is making a cake upstairs, and their father is downstairs making chocolate.

Fais do - do, Co - las mon petit frè - re,
fai doh - doh koh - la mon ptee freh - ruh

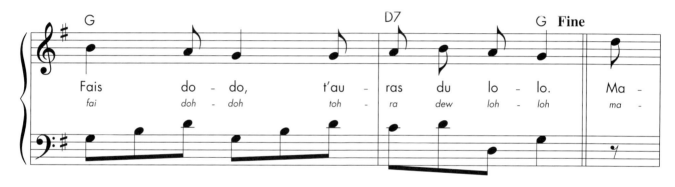

Fais do - do, t'au - ras du lo - lo. Ma -
fai doh - doh toh - ra dew loh - loh ma -

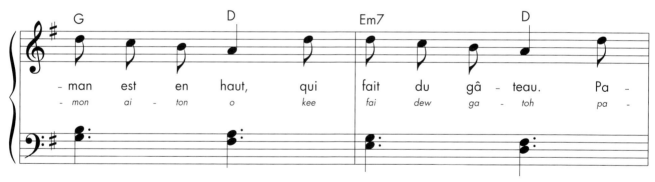

- man est en haut, qui fait du gâ - teau. Pa -
- mon ai - ton o kee fai dew ga - toh pa -

- pa est en bas, qui fait du lo - la.
- pa ai - ton ba kee fai dew loh - la

D.C. al fine

12

Dimanche matin
Sunday morning

On Sunday morning, the Emperor, his wife and the prince visit the singer to shake his hand. When they find he is not at home, the prince says "Never mind, we'll come back on Monday."

dimanche
lundi
mardi
mercredi
jeudi
vendredi
samedi

Sing this seven times, once for each day of the week.

Here are the days of the week in French.

Di - manche ma - tin, l'em - pereur, sa femme et le petit prin - ce,
dee - monsh ma - tan lom - pruhr sa fam ai luh ptee pran - suh

Sont ve - nus chez moi, pour me ser - rer la pin - ce.
son vuh - new shai mwa poor muh seh - rai la pan - suh

Comme j'é - tais par - ti, le petit prince a dit:
com jai - tai pah - tee luh ptee pranse a dee

Ça ne fait rien, nous re - vien - drons lun - di.
sa nuh fai reean noo ruh - vyon - dron lan - dee

La capucine
Nasturtium dance

This song was first sung late in the 18th century. At that time, many people in France were very poor and did not have enough to eat. U*ne capucine* is a kind of flower. In English it is called a nasturtium.

The singers dance *la capucine* to cheer themselves up when they have no bread.

There is bread at the house next door, but it is not for them.

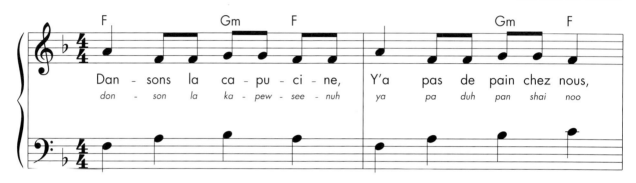

Dan - sons la ca - pu - ci - ne,
don - son la ka - pew - see - nuh

Y'a pas de pain chez nous,
ya pa duh pan shai noo

Y'en a chez la voi - si - ne,
yon - na shai la vwa - zee - nuh

Mais ce n'est pas pour nous.
mai suh nai pa poor noo

Piou!
pyoo

Dansons la capucine
don-son la ka-pew-see-nuh
Y'a du plaisir chez nous
ya dew plai-zeer shai noo
On pleure chez la voisine,
on pluhr shai la vwa-zee-nuh
On rit toujours chez nous. Piou!
on ree too-joor shai noo pyoo

Dancing *la capucine* makes them happy. They are always laughing, even though they are hungry.

Despite having bread, people are crying at the house next door.

① While you sing this song, dance around in a circle.

② Shout *Piou!* at the end of each verse, and jump in the air.

Piou!

③ When you land, crouch down.

④ When you begin the next verse, stand up straight again.

Savez-vous planter les choux?

Do you know how to plant cabbages?

There are actions to go with this song. You have to sing it several times and use a different action each time. It will help you remember the French words for parts of your body.

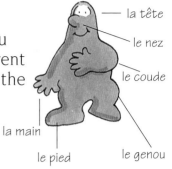

- la tête
- le nez
- le coude
- la main
- le pied
- le genou

A la mode de chez nous means "Like we do at home".

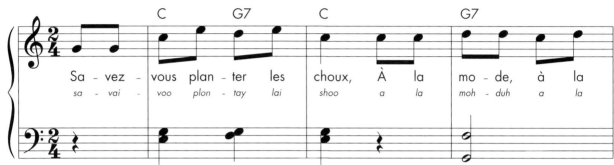

C G7 C G7

Sa - vez - vous plan - ter les choux, À la mo - de, à la
sa - vai - voo plon - tay lai shoo a la moh - duh a la

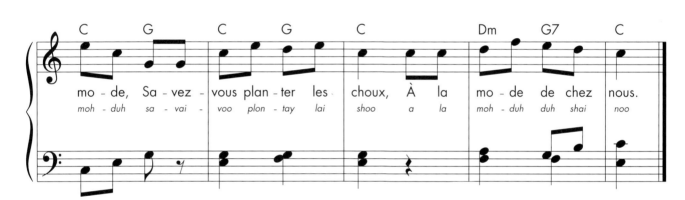

C G C G C Dm G7 C

mo - de, Sa - vez - vous plan - ter les choux, À la mo - de de chez nous.
moh - duh sa - vai - voo plon - tay lai shoo a la moh - duh duh shai noo

On les plante avec les pieds,
on lai plon-ta-vek lai peeai
À la mode, à la mode,
a la moh-duh a la moh-duh
On les plante avec les pieds,
on lai plon-ta-vek lai peeai
À la mode de chez nous.
a la moh-duh duh shai noo

Avec les pieds means "with our feet". Pretend you are digging a hole in the ground with your foot.

Sing the second verse a few times, but name a different part of the body each time. Do the actions too, for these words:

. . . *avec le coude*
a-vek luh kood

. . . *avec le genou*
a-vek luh jnoo

. . . *avec la main*
a-vek la man

. . . *avec le nez*
a-vek luh nai

15

Promenons-nous dans les bois

Let's go walking in the woods

The songs on these pages have games to go with them. For this one, you have to go walking in the woods without being caught and eaten by the wolf.

Choose one person to be the wolf.

The others dance around the wolf in a circle and sing the song.

Prome - nons - nous dans les bois
prom - non - noo don lai bwa

pen - dant que le loup n'y est pas,
pon - don kuh luh loo neeai pa

Si le loup y é - tait,
see luh loo ee ai - tai

il nous man - ge - rait,
eel noo mon - juh - rai

Mais comme il n'y est pas,
mai com eel neeai pa

il nous man - gera pas.
eel noo mon - jra pa

Loup y es-tu?
loo yeh - tew
(Loup : "Oui!")
wee

Que fais- tu?
kuh fay - tew
(Loup : "Je mets ma culotte!")
juh may ma kew - lot

① Speak the words *Loup y es-tu* (Wolf, are you there?), don't sing them. When the wolf says *Oui*, the others ask *Que fais-tu?* (What are you doing?).

② The wolf says *Je mets ma culotte* (I'm putting on my trousers).

③ Sing the song a few more times. Each time, the wolf names a different piece of clothing in the last bar:

. . . Je mets mes chaussettes (sho-sett).

. . . Je mets mon chapeau (sha-po).

. . . Je mets ma veste (vest).

④ Finally, when he is asked *Que fais-tu?*, the wolf says *J'arrive* (ja-reev), which means "I'm coming", and chases the others.

⑤ The person he catches then becomes the wolf, and the game begins again.

Le furet

The ferret

One player is "it", and walks around the back of the circle, holding a toy animal (the *furet*). She drops it behind one player's back, trying to make sure nobody sees.

A ferret is a small furry animal that runs very fast.

You sit in a circle to play this game.

Il court il court le fu - ret, Le fu - ret du bois mes -
eel koor eel koor luh few - rai luh few - rai dew bwa mai -

- dames, Il court il court le fu - ret, Le fu - ret du bois jo -
- dam eel koor eel koor luh few - rai luh few - rai dew bwa jo -

- li. Il est pas - sé par i - ci, Il re - pas - se - ra par là.
- lee eel ai pas - say pahr ee - see eel ruh - pas - suh - ra pahr la

① When the song is finished, the players look behind them for the *furet*.

② The player who finds the *furet* picks it up and chases the person who is "it" around the circle.

③ If the person who is "it" reaches the gap in the circle before she is caught, she sits down.

④ The player left standing becomes "it", and the game begins again.

⑤ If "it" is caught before she reaches the gap, she is "it" for another turn.

Frère Jacques

Brother James

This song is about a monk who has slept too late. *Matines* are prayers that monks say very early in the morning. *Sonnez les matines* means "Ring the bells to call the monks to morning prayers".

The singer asks Frère Jacques
Dormez-vous? (Are you sleeping?).

Frère is the word for brother. It is also the word for a monk.

Frè - re Jac - ques,
freh - ruh ja - kuh

Frè - re Jac - ques
freh - ruh ja - kuh

Dor - mez - vous?
door - mai - voo

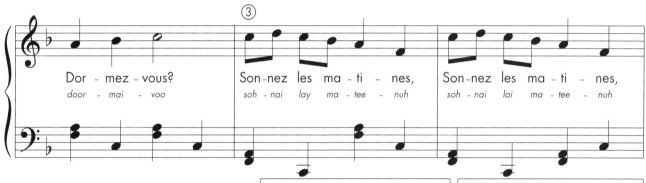

Dor - mez - vous?
door - mai - voo

Son - nez les ma - ti - nes,
soh - nai lay ma - tee - nuh

Son - nez les ma - ti - nes,
soh - nai lai ma - tee - nuh

Ding, Dingue, Dong,
deeng dang dong

Ding, Dingue, Dong,
deeng dang dong

Ding, Dingue, Dong
deeng dang dong

Ding, Dingue, Dong is an imitation of the sound of bells.

Try singing this tune as a round. Three or four people or groups are best, though it will work with two as well.

The second singer starts at the beginning when the first reaches the 2 in the music.

The third singer starts when the first reaches the number 3. The fourth singer begins when the first reaches the number 4.

If there are only two singers, the second can begin when the first reaches either the number 2 or the number 3.

Meunier, tu dors

Miller, you're sleeping

In this song, the singer is trying to wake the miller up to tell him that his mill is going too quickly.

Un moulin is a mill that grinds wheat into flour.

In the past, mills were usually powered by water or wind.

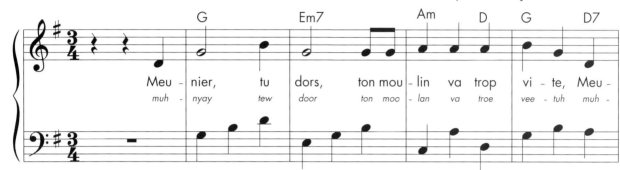

Meu - nier, tu dors, ton mou - lin va trop vi - te, Meu -
muh - nyay tew door ton moo - lan va troe vee - tuh muh -

- nier, tu dors, ton mou - lin va trop fort. Ton mou - lin, ton mou - lin va trop
- nyay tew door ton moo - lan va troe for ton moo - lan ton moo - lan va trop

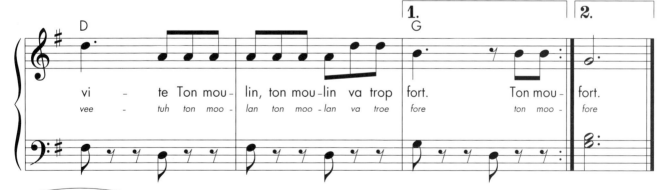

vi - te Ton mou - lin, ton mou - lin va trop fort. Ton mou - fort.
vee - tuh ton moo - lan ton moo - lan va troe fore ton moo - fore

When you sing the second part of the song, you have to get faster.

À la meunière is a popular method of cooking fish in France.

The fish is coated in flour, then fried in butter. When it is cooked, lemon juice is added.

Une meunière is a miller's wife, who would have had plenty of flour to use in the recipe.

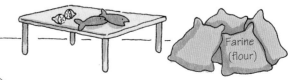

Farine (flour)

Cadet Rousselle

Cadet Rousselle

This is a nonsense song. Cadet Rousselle's three houses have no beams or rafters. He uses them as a home for swallows.

Que direz-vous d'Cadet Rousselle means "What do you think of Cadet Rousselle?".

Cadet Rousselle est bon enfant means "Cadet Rousselle is a nice fellow".

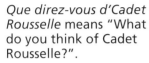

Ca-det Rous-selle a trois mai - sons, Ca-det Rous- selle a trois mai -
ka - dai roo - sel a trwa mai - zon ka - dai roo - sel a trwa mai -

- sons, Qui n'ont ni pou - tres ni che - vrons, Qui n'ont ni pou - tres ni che -
- zon kee non nee poo - truh nee shuh - vron kee non nee poo - truh nee shuh -

- vrons, C'est pour lo - ger les hi - ron - del - les, Que di - rez - vous d'Ca - det Rous -
- vron sai poor lo - jai lai zee - ron - del - luh kuh dee - rai - voo dka - dai roo -

- sel - le, Ah, ah, ah, oui vrai - ment, Ca-det Rous-selle est bon en - fant!
- sel - luh ah ah ah we vrai - mon ka - dai roo - sel ai bon on - fon

20

Here are the other verses to the song.

As in the first verse, you have to sing the first line twice, then repeat the second line too.

① *Un habit* means "clothing". Cadet Rousselle has two sets of yellow clothes.

Cadet Rousselle a trois habits,
ka-dai roo-sel a trwa za-bee
Deux jaunes et l'autre en papier gris,
duh jone ai lo-tron pa-pyai gree
Il met celui-la quand il gèle,
eel mai suh-lwee-la kon-teel jel-luh
Ou quand il pleut, et quand il grêle,
oo kon-teel pluh ai kon-teel grel-luh
Ah, ah, ah, oui vraiment,
ah ah ah we vrai-mon
Cadet Rousselle est bon enfant!
ka-dai roo-sel ai bon on-fon

② His third set of clothes is made of grey paper. He wears them when it freezes, rains or hails.

③ *Celui-la* means "that one". Sometimes you will hear *celui-ci*, too, which means "this one".

Cadet Rousselle a trois garçons,
ka-dai roo-sel a trwa gar-son
L'un est voleur, l'autre est fripon,
lan ai vo-luhr lo-trai free-pon
Le troisième est un peu ficelle,
luh trwa-zyem ai-tan puh fi-sel-luh
Il ressemble à Cadet Rousselle,
eel ruh-son-bla ka-dai roo-sel-luh
Ah, ah, ah, oui vraiment,
ah ah ah we vrai-mon
Cadet Rousselle est bon enfant!
ka-dai roo-sel ai bon on-fon

Mon frère cadet means "My younger brother".

Un cadet is a young soldier.

④ Cadet Rousselle has three sons. One is a thief, another is a rascal.

⑤ The third is a bit sneaky. He is rather like Cadet Rousselle.

Ficelle is also the French word for string.

Il pleut, il pleut bergère

Shepherdess, it's raining

This song was written in the 1790s. At that time, many rich people thought it was fashionable to dress as shepherds and shepherdesses. Songs and plays about the countryside became very popular.

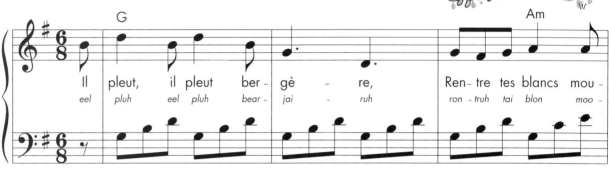

G | Am

Il pleut, il pleut ber — gè — re, Ren— tre tes blancs mou—
eel pluh eel pluh bear — jai — ruh ron — truh tai blon moo —

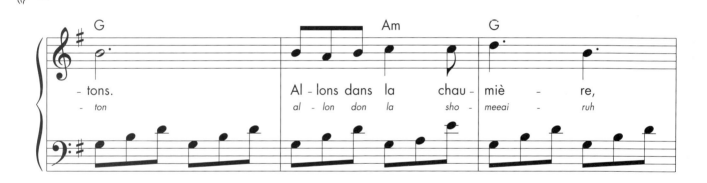

G | Am | G

— tons. Al — lons dans la chau — miè — re,
— ton al — lon don la sho — meeai — ruh

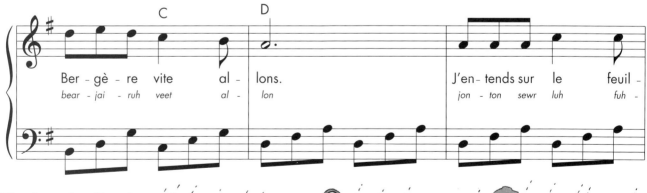

C | D

Ber — gè — re vite al — lons. J'en— tends sur le feuil —
bear — jai — ruh veet al — lon jon — ton sewr luh fuh —

①The singer is telling the shepherdess that it is raining and she must bring her sheep inside.

②He can hear the noise of the rain in the trees, and see the lightning flashing.

Entends-tu le tonnerre, il gronde en approchant.
on-ton-tew luh ton-nair-ruh eel grond on a-pro-shon
Prends un abri bergère, à ma droite en marchant.
pron-dan a-bree bear-jai-ruh a ma drwat on mar-shon
Voilà notre cabane, et tiens voici venir
vwa-la no-truh ka-bah-nuh ai tian vwa-see vuh-neer
Ma mère et ma soeur Anne, qui vont l'étable ouvrir.
ma mair ai ma sur an-nuh kee von lai-tah-bloo-vreer

③ He asks if the shepherdess can hear the thunder rumbling, and invites her to come with him to his family's hut.

④ He tells her he can see his mother and his sister Anne opening the stable.

G	C	D
la - ge,	L'eau qui tombe à grand bruit.	Voi -
- ya - juh	lo key tom - ba gron brwee	vwa -

rit.

G	C	D7	G
ci ve - nir l'o - ra - ge,		Voi - là l'é - clair qui	luit._____
- see vuh - neer lo - ra - juh		vwa - la lai - klair kee	lwee

Bonsoir, bonsoir ma mère, ma soeur Anne bonsoir.
bon-swar bon-swar ma mair-uh ma sur an-nuh bon-swar
J'amène ma bergère, près de vous pour ce soir.
ja-mei-nuh ma bear-jai-ruh preh duh voo poor suh swar
Va te sécher ma mie, auprès de nos tisons.
va tuh sai-shai ma mee-uh oh-preh duh no tee-zon
Soeur fais-lui compagnie, entrez petits moutons!
suhr fai-lwee com-pa-nee-uh on-trai puh-tee moo-ton

⑤ The singer brings the shepherdess into the hut and tells her to get dry by the fire.

⑥ He asks his sister to keep the shepherdess company . . .

⑦ . . . and directs the sheep into the stable.

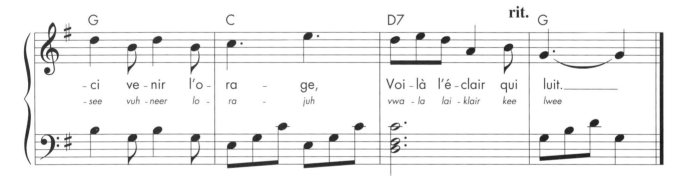

Ma mie is old French for "my friend".

23

Trois jeunes tambours

Three drummer boys

In the past, armies often had drummers to help the soldiers march in time. This song is about a young drummer boy who returns from battle and falls in love with the king's daughter.

Trois jeunes tam-bours s'en re-ve-naient de guer - re,
trwa juhn tom - boor son ruh - vuh - nai duh gai - ruh

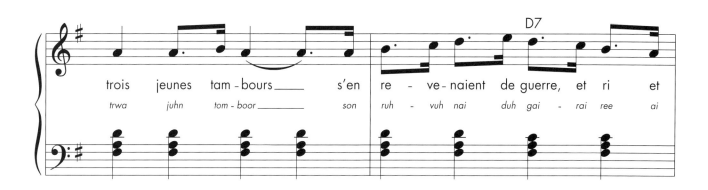

trois jeunes tam-bours s'en re-ve-naient de guerre, et ri et
trwa juhn tom - boor son ruh - vuh nai duh gai - rai ree ai

ran ra-pa-ta-plan! s'en re-ve-naient de guer - re.
ran ra - pa - ta - plan son ruh - vuh - nai duh gai - ruh.

Tambour is the word for a drummer boy, and also for a type of drum.

Et ri et ran ra pa ta plan is an imitation of the sound the drum makes.

Here are the extra verses. Sing each line twice, then *Et ri et ran ra pa ta plan,* followed by the last half of the line.

① The youngest drummer boy has a rose in his mouth.

Le plus jeune a dans sa bouche une rose
luh plew juhn a don sa boosh ew-nuh ro-zuh

La fille du roi était à sa fenêtre
la fee dew rwa et-tai-ta sa fuh-neh-truh

② As he marches by, the princess asks for the rose.

Joli tambour, donne-moi donc ta rose
jo-lee tom-boor don-nuh-mwa donk ta roz-uh

Fille du roi, donne-moi donc ton coeur
fee-uh dew rwa don-nuh-mwa donk ton kuhr

③ The drummer boy asks the princess to marry him. She tells him to ask her father, the king.

④ The king says the drummer boy is not rich enough to marry his daughter.

Joli tambour, demande-le à mon père
jo-lee tom-boor duh-mond-luh a mon pear-uh

Sire le roi, donnez-moi votre fille
see-ruh luh rwa don-nai-mwa voh-truh fee-uh

Joli tambour, tu n'es pas assez riche
jo-lee tom-boor tew nai pa-za-sai ree-shuh

⑤ The drummer says he has ships on the sea loaded with gold and jewels.

J'ai des vaisseaux, dessus la mer jolie
jai dai vess-oh duh-sue la mare jo-lee-uh

L'un chargé d'or, l'autre de pierreries
lan shar-jai door loh-truh duh pyair-uh-ree-uh

Joli tambour, tu auras donc ma fille
jo-lee tom-boor tew or-a donk ma fee-uh

⑥ The king allows him to marry the princess.

Dans mon pays, il y en a de plus jolies
don mon pay lyon-na duh plew jo-lee-uh

⑦ But the drummer says he no longer wants to marry her, as there are prettier women in his own country.

Il est né, le divin enfant

The divine child is born

This song is a Christmas carol, about the birth of Jesus. The music on this page is a chorus. Sing it before and after the music opposite.

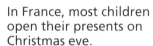

In France, most children open their presents on Christmas eve.

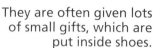

They are often given lots of small gifts, which are put inside shoes.

Il est né le di - vin en - fant,
eel *ai* *nai* *luh* *dee -* *vee -* *non -* *fon*

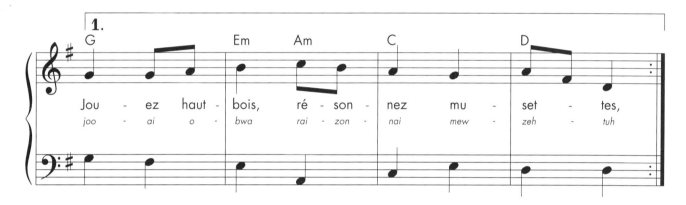

1.

Jou - ez haut - bois, ré - son - nez mu - set - tes,
joo *- ai* *o -* *bwa* *rai - zon -* *nai* *mew -* *zeh -* *tuh*

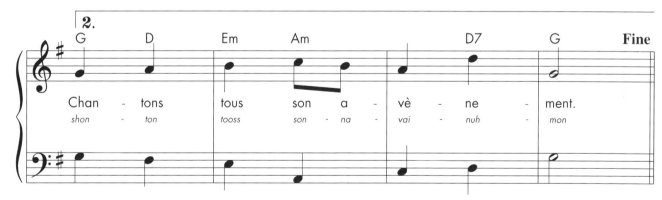

2.

Chan - tons tous son a - vè - ne - ment.
shon *- ton* *tooss* *son - na -* *vai -* *nuh -* *mon*

Fine

Hautbois are oboes. *Musettes* are a kind of bagpipes.

Jouez and *résonnez* are words commanding the instruments to start playing.

Chantons tous son avènement means "Let's all sing to celebrate his arrival".

Les prophètes are the prophets, who promised the baby's arrival.

Depuis plus de quatre mille ans means "for more than four thousand years".

Nous attendions cet heureux temps means "we have waited for this happy time".

C   G

De - puis plus de qua - tre mille ans,
duh - pwee plew duh kah - truh mee - lon

1.   Am   D

Nous le pro - met - taient les pro - phè - tes,
noo luh pro - meh - tai lai pro - fet - tuh

G   Am   D

2.

Nous at - tend - ions cet heu - reux temps.
noo - za - ton - dyon set uh - ruh ton

D.C. al fine

The words on the right are the second verse, which you sing to the music on this page. Then sing the chorus one last time.

Une étable est son logement
ewn ai-tah-blai son lo-juh-mon
Un peu de paille est sa couchette
an puh duh pie ai sa coo-shet-tuh
Une étable est son logement
ewn ai-tah-blai son lo-juh-mon
Pour un Dieu quel abaissement!
poor an diuh kel a-bes-suh-mon

This verse is about Jesus being born in a stable, on a mattress of straw.

Les trois rois

The three kings

This is an old Christmas song from Provence in the south of France. It tells the story of the three kings on their way to see the baby Jesus.

Un train is a train, but it also means a procession.

The singer describes the procession of the kings.

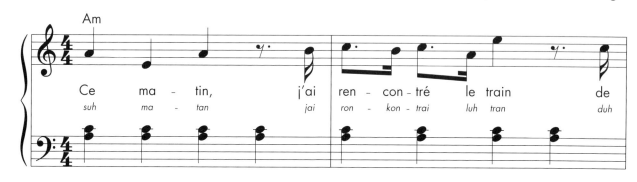

Am

Ce ma- tin, j'ai ren- con- tré le train de
suh ma- tan jai ron- kon-trai luh tran duh

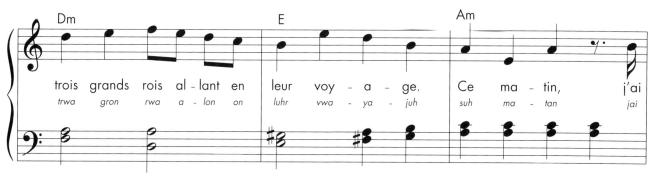

Dm   E   Am

trois grands rois al- lant en leur voy- a- ge. Ce ma- tin, j'ai
trwa gron rwa a- lon on luhr vwa- ya- juh suh ma- tan jai

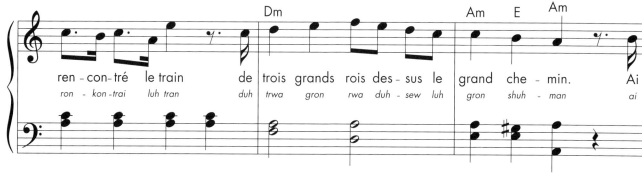

Dm   Am   E   Am

ren- con-tré le train de trois grands rois des- sus le grand che- min. Ai
ron- kon-trai luh tran duh trwa gron rwa duh-sew luh gron shuh- man ai

At Christmastime in Provence, many people make *crèches de Noël*, models of the stable where Jesus was born.

They make or buy *santons*, small models of people and animals.

Santons are brightly painted, or dressed in very detailed costumes.

① When you get to the end of the song, sing the words and music opposite again.

② Finish by singing the extra words, shown here, to the music on this page.

Et les tambours pour leur faire honneur
ai lai tom-boor poor luhr fair on-nurr
de temps en temps faisaient taire leur tapage.
duh ton-zon ton fuh-zai tare luhr ta-pah-juh
Et les tambours pour leur faire honneur
ai lai tom-boor poor luhr fair on-nurr
battaient la marche chacun à leur tour.
bat-teh la marsh-uh sha-kan a luhr toor

③ This verse says that the drummers stopped playing from time to time in praise of the kings. Then they took turns beating a march.

Word list

Here is a list of French words and phrases that you will find in this book. All the nouns (naming words) have *le, la, l'* or *les* in front of them, which means "the". Some French adjectives (describing words) change depending on the type of nouns they are describing. In this list, the adjectives are shown as they appear in the songs, but sometimes the variations are given too.

Some of the words and phrases in the songs mean more than one thing, or have an old-fashioned meaning and a modern one. This list tells you the meanings of the words as they are used in the songs.

à - at, to
à grand bruit - with a lot of noise
à leur tour - in turn
à ma droite - on my right
l'abri - shelter
aimer - to like, to love
aller (allant; allons) - to go (going; let's go)
l'alouette - skylark
amener (j'amène) - to bring (I'm bringing)
l'ami/l'amie - friend (male/female)
l'amour - love
l'an - year
approcher - to come near
arriver - to arrive, to come
assez - enough
attendre (nous attendions) - to wait for (we were waiting for)
auprès de - near
l'autre - the other one
avoir (j'ai; il a) - to have (I have; he has)

battre (ils battaient) - to beat (they were beating)
beau(x)/bel(le) - beautiful, handsome
la bergère - shepherdess
bien - a lot, well
blanc(he) - white
les bois - woods
bon(ne) - good
bonsoir - good evening
la bouche - mouth
le briquet - lighter

ça ne fait rien - it doesn't matter
la cabane - hut
car - because
ce/cet/cette - this, that
c'est (ce n'est pas) - it is (it isn't)
celui-là/celle-là - that one
la cerise - cherry
chacun(e) - each one
la chandelle - candle
chanter (chantons) - to sing (let's sing)
le chapeau - hat
chargé(e) de - loaded with
la chaumière - cottage
la chaussette - sock
le chemin - path
le chêne - oak tree

le chevron - rafter
chez moi/nous - at *or* to my/our house
le chou - cabbage
cinq - five
clair(e) - bright, clear
le clair de (la) lune - moonlight
le coeur - heart
comme - as, like
comme ci - like this
comme ça - like that
le coquelicot - poppy
la couchette - somewhere to sleep, berth (in a train)
le coucou - cuckoo
le coude - elbow
courir (il court) - to run (he is running)
croire (je crois) - to think, to believe (I think, I believe)
cueillir - to gather, to pick
la cuisine - kitchen
la culotte - trousers

d'abord - at first
dans - in, into
danser - to dance
le dauphin - dolphin
le Dauphin - prince who will become king
de temps en temps - from time to time
demander - to ask
depuis - since, for
descendre - to go down
dessus - over, on top of
deux - two
dieu - god
dimanche - Sunday
dire - to say
divin(e) - divine
dix - ten
donc - so
donne-moi - give me
donner - to give
doré(e) - golden
dormir (dormez-vous?) - to sleep (are you sleeping?)
douze - twelve

l'eau - water
l'éclair - flash of lightning
écrire - to write
elle - she, it

elle y est - she is there
l'empereur - emperor
en bas - low down, downstairs
en haut - high up, upstairs
en rond - in a circle
l'enfant - child
entendre (entends-tu?) - to hear (can you hear?)
entrer (entrez) - to come in (come in)
est - is
est né - is born
et - and
l'étable - stable
être (elle était) - to be (she was)

faire - to do, to make
faire honneur - to praise
faire taire - to stop (a noise)
fais dodo - go to sleep (children's language)
fais-lui compagnie - keep her company
la femme - woman, wife
la fenêtre - window
le feu - fire, flame
le feuillage - foliage
la fille - daughter
la fontaine - fountain, natural spring
la forêt - forest
fort - hard, loud, strong
le frère - brother
le fripon - rascal

le garçon - boy
le garde du corps - guardsman
le gâteau - cake
le genou - knee
gentil(le) - sweet, kind
grand(e) - big, large, great
gris(e) - grey
gronder - to roar
la guerre - war

l'habit - set of clothes
haut - high
heureux/heureuse - happy
le hibou - owl
l'hirondelle - swallow
huit - eight

ici - here
il - he, it
il gèle - it's freezing
il grêle - it's hailing

il pleut - it's raining
il y a - there is, there are

jamais - never
le jardin - garden
jaune - yellow
je - I
je n'ai plus de - I no longer have any
je suis - I am
jeudi - Thursday
jeune - young
joli(e) - pretty
jouer - to play

là - there
leur - (to) them, their
le lit - bed
le logement - accommodation
loger - to lodge
lointain(e) - distant
longtemps - for a long time
le loup - wolf
luire (luit) - to shine (shines)

la main - hand
mais - but
la maison - house
maman - mum, mom
manger - to eat
  (*il [ne] nous mangera pas; il nous mangerait* - he won't eat us; he would eat us)
la marche - march
marcher (en marchant) - to walk (walking)
mardi - Tuesday
le matin - morning
la mer - sea
mercredi - Wednesday
la mère - mother
mesdames - ladies
messieurs - gentlemen
mettre - to put on (clothes)
le meunier - miller
mille - thousand
mon/ma/mes - my
mort(e) - dead, finished
le mot - word, short letter
le moulin - mill
le mouton - sheep

ne (n')... pas - not
ne (n')... plus - not any more
neuf - nine
neuf - new
le nez - nose
ni... ni - neither... nor
notre/nos - our
nous - we, us
nouveau/nouvelle - new
n'y est pas - isn't here, isn't there

onze - eleven
l'or - gold

l'orage - storm
ou - or
oublier - to forget
oui - yes
ouvre-moi - open (the door) for me
ouvrir - to open

le page - page boy
la paille - straw
le pain - bread
le panier - basket
papa - dad
le papier - paper
par - through
partir - to go away
passer - to go through
  (*il est passé; il passera* - he went through; he will go through)
le pays - country
pendant que - while
le père - father
petit(e) - little
le pied - foot
les pierreries - precious stones
le plaisir - pleasure, happiness
planter - to plant
pleurer - to cry
il pleut - it is raining
la plume - feather, pen
plumer - to pluck (feathers)
plus - more
le pont - bridge
la porte - door
pour - for
la poutre - beam
prendre - to take
près de - near
prête-moi - lend me
prince - prince
promettaient - were promising
promettre - to promise
p'tit - short for *petit*

quand - when
quatre - four
qui - who, which
que - that
que direz-vous? - what will you say?
que fais-tu? - what are you doing ?
quel - what (a)

rencontrer (j'ai rencontré) - to meet (I met)
rentrer - to take in, to bring inside
répondre (il répondit) - to answer (he answered)
ressembler à - to look like
rester - to remain, to stay
revenir - to come back
rêver - to dream
riche - rich
rire - to laugh
le roi - king
le romarin - rosemary

rond - round
la rose - rose
rouge - red

samedi - Saturday
savez-vous? - do you know how to?
savoir - to know
se baigner - to swim, to bathe
se promener - to go for a walk
se rendormir (il se rendort) - to go back to sleep (he goes back to sleep)
se sécher - to dry oneself
s'en revenaient - were coming back
sept - seven
serrer la pince - to shake someone's hand (slang)
si - so
sire - sire
six - six
la soeur - sister
le soir - evening
son/sa/ses - his, her
sur - on, upon

le tambour - drummer boy *or* drum
le tapage - noise
t'auras - you shall have
le temps - time
la tête - head
le tison - brand
tomber - to fall
ton/ta/tes - your
le tonnerre - thunder
toujours - always
tout(e)/tous - all
le train - train, procession, line
trois - three
troisième - third
trop - too much
la troupe - group
trouver - to find
tu - you

un/une - a
un peu de - a little

va chez - go to
le vaisseau - ship
vendredi - Friday
venir - to come
la veste - jacket
vite - quick(ly)
voici - here is, here are
voilà - there is, there are
voir (j'ai vu) - to see (I saw)
le voleur - thief
le voyage - journey
vous - you
vraiment - really

y'en a - there is some

Singing French songs

If you read them as if they were English words, the pronunciation guides in the songs will help you to sound French. But some letters in French do not have the same sounds as they do in English, so you have to say them differently. Here are some extra tips about a few of the most important ones.

In French, you say the letter ¨r¨ at the back of your mouth, as if you were gargling.

The letter ¨u¨ in words like **tu** is shown in the pronunciation guides as ¨ew¨. To say this properly, make a circle with your lips as if you were saying ¨oo¨, then try to say ¨ee¨.

The French ¨j¨ in words like **jeune** sounds like the letter ¨s¨ in the English word ¨treasure¨.

If you follow the pronunciation guides, you may notice that you often have to sing words in French differently from the way you would speak them. You have to make certain parts of words sound more important, particularly endings. For example, for the word **rose** you would say ¨roz¨, but you have to sing ¨ro-zuh¨. You also run words together more than when you speak, so that **gens armés** becomes ¨jon-zahr-mai¨ when you sing it.

This is partly because in French, as in many other languages, singers change the words to make them fit properly with the music. Also, many of the songs are very old, so you may be singing words and phrases that French people would not normally say today.

Listen to these tunes on the Internet

If you have a computer, you can listen to all the tunes to these songs on the Usborne Quicklinks Website to hear how they go. At Usborne Quicklinks you will also find a virtual keyboard which you can use to play simple tunes on your computer. Just go to **www.usborne-quicklinks.com** and enter the keywords "French Songbook", then follow the simple instructions.

Guitar chords

The diagrams on the right show you how to play all the chords you need for this book.

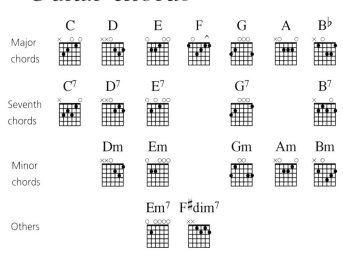

This edition first published in 2003 by Usborne Publishing, Usborne House, 83-85 Saffron Hill, London EC1N 8RT, England. Copyright © 2003, 1995 Usborne Publishing Ltd. First published in America March 1996.